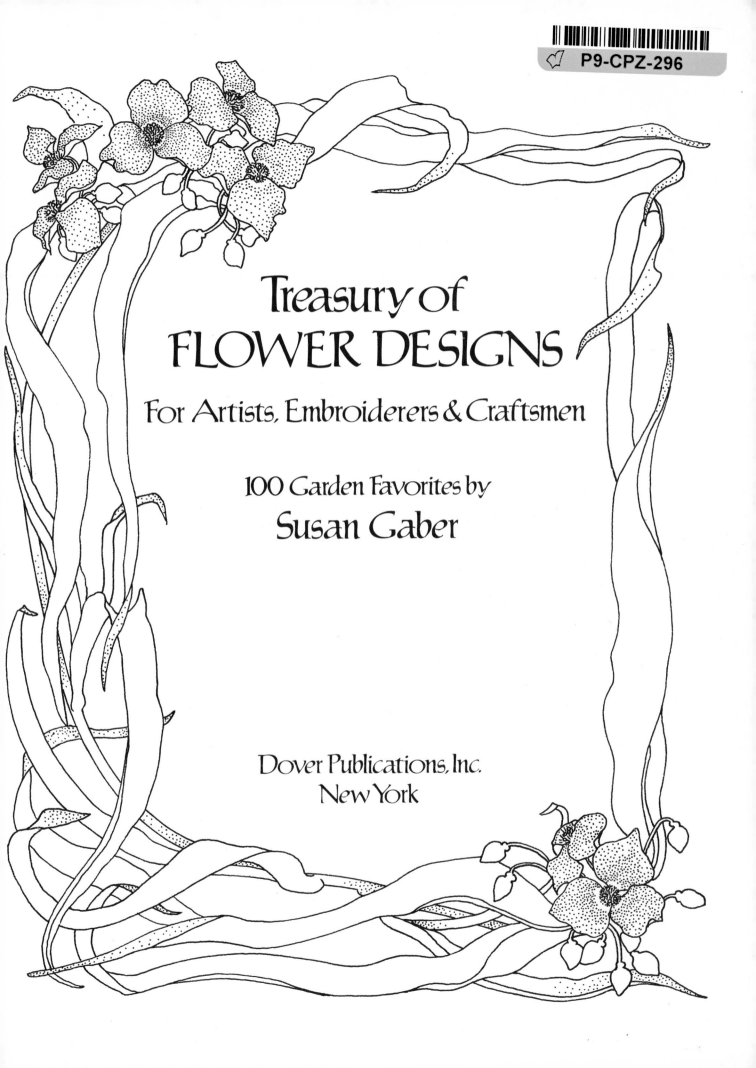

Treasury of FLOWER DESIGNS

For Artists, Embroiderers & Craftsmen

100 Garden Favorites by
Susan Gaber

Dover Publications, Inc.
New York

Copyright © 1981 by Susan Gaber.
All rights reserved under Pan American and International Copyright Conventions.

Published in Canada by General Publishing Company, Ltd., 30 Lesmill Road, Don Mills, Toronto, Ontario.
Published in the United Kingdom by Constable and Company, Ltd., 10 Orange Street, London WC2H 7EG.

Treasury of Flower Designs for Artists, Embroiderers and Craftsmen is a new work, first published by Dover Publications, Inc., in 1981.

DOVER *Pictorial Archive* SERIES

Treasury of Flower Designs for Artists, Embroiderers and Craftsmen belongs to the Dover Pictorial Archive Series. Up to ten illustrations from this book may be reproduced on any one project or in any single publication free and without special permission. Wherever possible please include a credit line indicating the title of the book, author and publisher. Please address the publisher for permission to make more extensive use of illustrations in this book than that authorized above.
The republication of this book in whole is prohibited.

International Standard Book Number:
0-486-24096-7
Library of Congress Catalog Card Number:
80-69296

Manufactured in the United States of America
Dover Publications, Inc.
180 Varick Street
New York, N.Y. 10014

Alphabetical List of Flowers Illustrated

African Violet, 42
Amaryllis, 62
Anemone, 3, 77
Anthurium, 39
Asarina, 50
Aster, 6

Begonia, 30, 39, 70
Black-eyed Susan, 32
Bleeding Heart, 69

Cactus, Christmas, 38
Cactus, Orchid, 18
Calendula, 22
Calla Lily, 64
Camellia, 77
Canterbury Bells, 61
Carnation, 11
Cherry, 29
Chrysanthemum, 72
Christmas Cactus, 38
Cinquefoil, 65
Clematis, 7
Clivia, 52
Columbine, 9
Coralbells, 43
Coreopsis, 58
Crocus, 32
Cyclamen, 39

Daffodil, 68, 77
Dahlia, 16, 19

Daisy, Shasta, 73
Daisy, Transvaal, 64
Day Lily, 76
Delphinium, 26
Dianthus, 54
Dogwood, 33

Edelweiss, 66

Flowering Quince, 40, 53
Flowering Tobacco, 33, 77
Forget-me-not, 38
Forsythia, 12
Foxglove, 51
Freesia, 56
Fritillaria, 38, 45
Fuchsia, 20, 27

Gardenia, 17
Gazania, 16
Geranium, 78
Geranium, Ivy, 41
Geum, 20
Gladiola, 24
Globe Flower, 12
Gloxinia, 48
Grape Hyacinth, 52

Helenium, 45
Helleborus, 12
Hibiscus, 25
Honeysuckle, 66
Hyacinth, 57

Hyacinth, Grape, 52
Hydrangea, 74

Impatiens, 4, 34
Iris, 47, 59
Ivy Geranium, 41

Layia, 54
Lilac, 8
Lilium, 55
Lily, 11
Lily, Calla, 64
Lily, Day, 76
Lily, Water, 41
Lily of the Valley, 70
Lychnis, 2

Magnolia, 30, 36
Marigold, 35
Morning Glory, 27

Narcissus, 63
Nasturtium, 37

Orchid, 14, 31, 52
Orchid Cactus, 18
Oxalis, 36

Pansy, 6
Peony (single), 15
Peony (double), 13
Petunia, 10, 33
Phlox, 65
Poinsettia, 52
Poppy, 12, 23

Portulaca, 24
Primrose, 44, 49

Quince, Flowering, 40, 53

Ranunculus, 48
Rhododendron, 37
Rose, 30, 46, 66, 71, 75
Rose of Sharon, 79

Scabiosa, 64
Shasta Daisy, 73
Snapdragon, 51
Snowdrop, 45
Spiderwort, 1
Strawflower, 48
Streptocarpus, 17
Sunflower, 48
Sweet Pea, 67

Thunbergia, 21
Tobacco, Flowering, 33, 77
Transvaal Daisy, 64
Tulip, 25, 28, 30

Verbena, 60
Viola, 69
Violet, African, 42

Water Lily, 41

Zinnia, 5

Impatiens

Zinnia

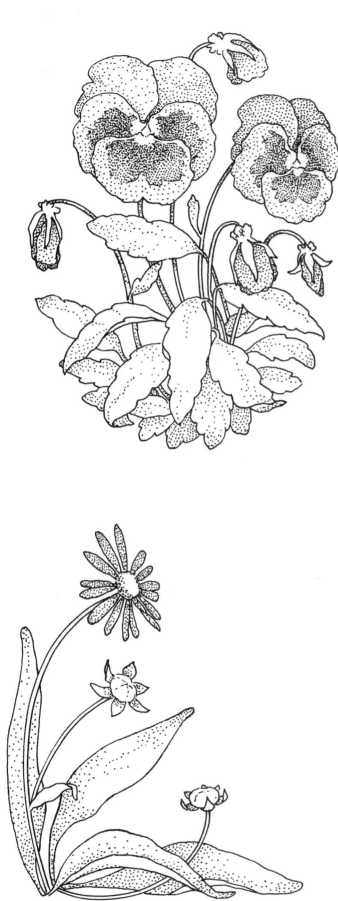

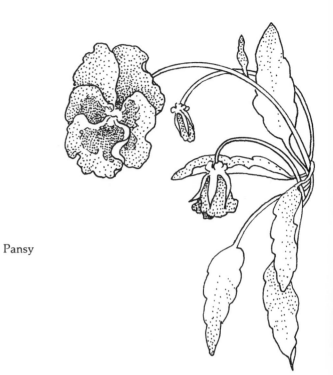

Pansy

Aster

Clematis

Lilac

Columbine

Petunia

Lily

Carnation

Globe Flower

Helleborus

Poppy

Forsythia

12

Peony (*single*)

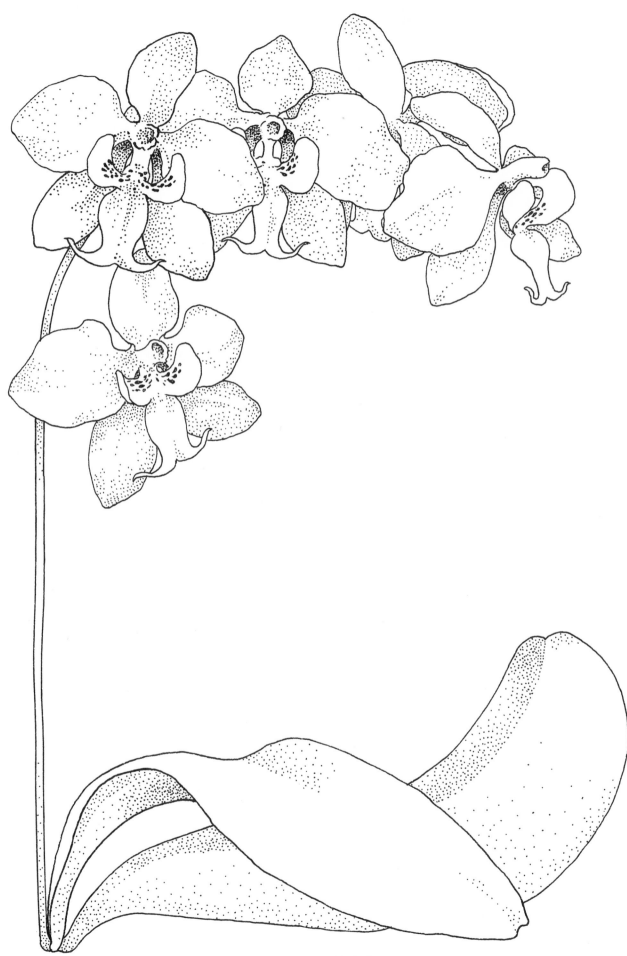

Orchid

Peony (*double*)

Dahlia

16

Gazania

Gardenia

Streptocarpus

Orchid Cactus

18

Dahlia

Fuchsia

Geum

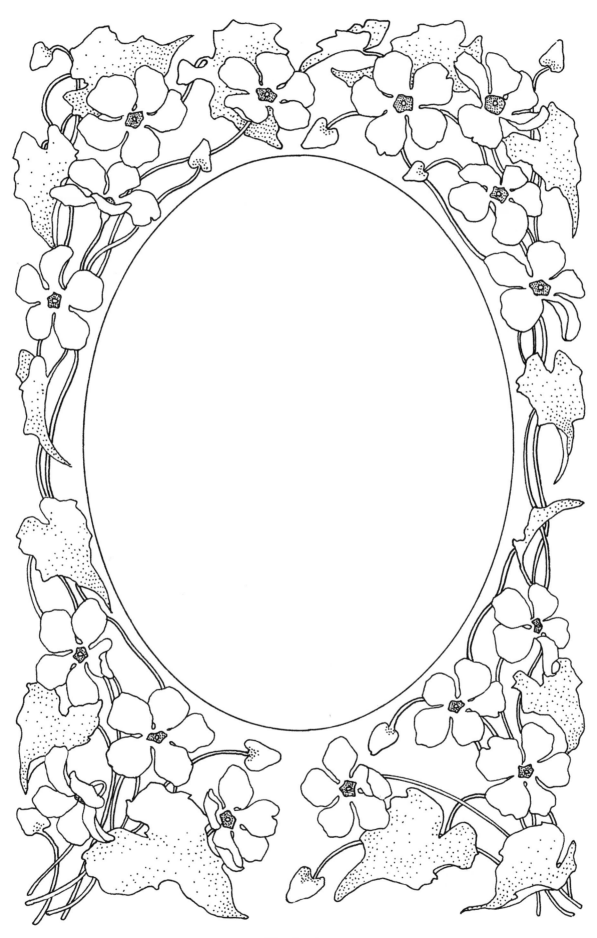

Thunbergia

Calendula

Poppy

23

Portulaca

Gladiola

Tulip

Hibiscus

Delphinium

Fuchsia

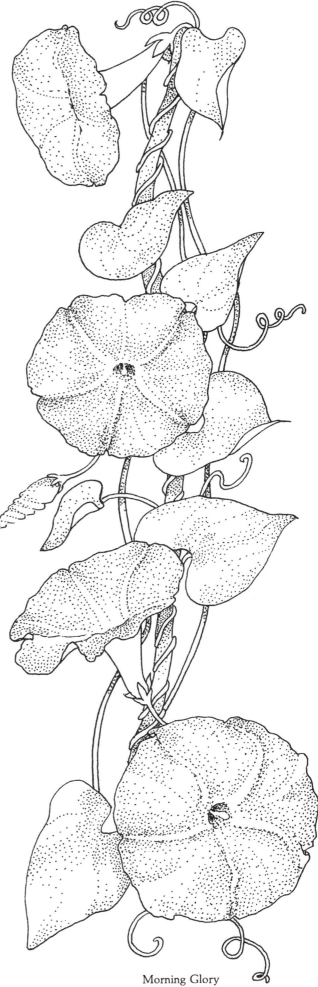

Morning Glory

Tulip

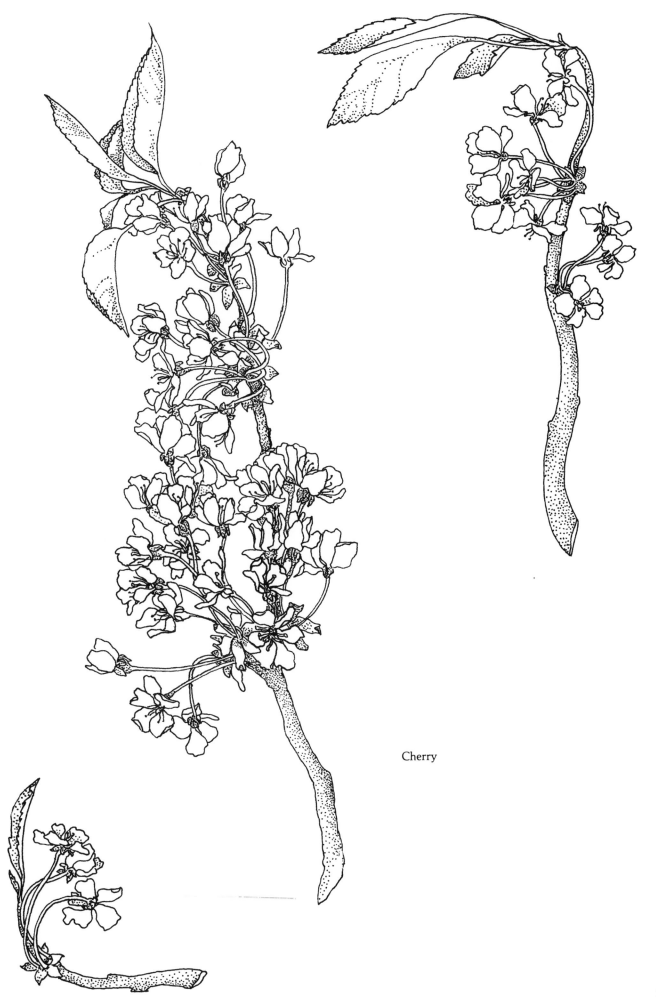

Cherry

Rose

Marigold

Begonia

Tulip

30

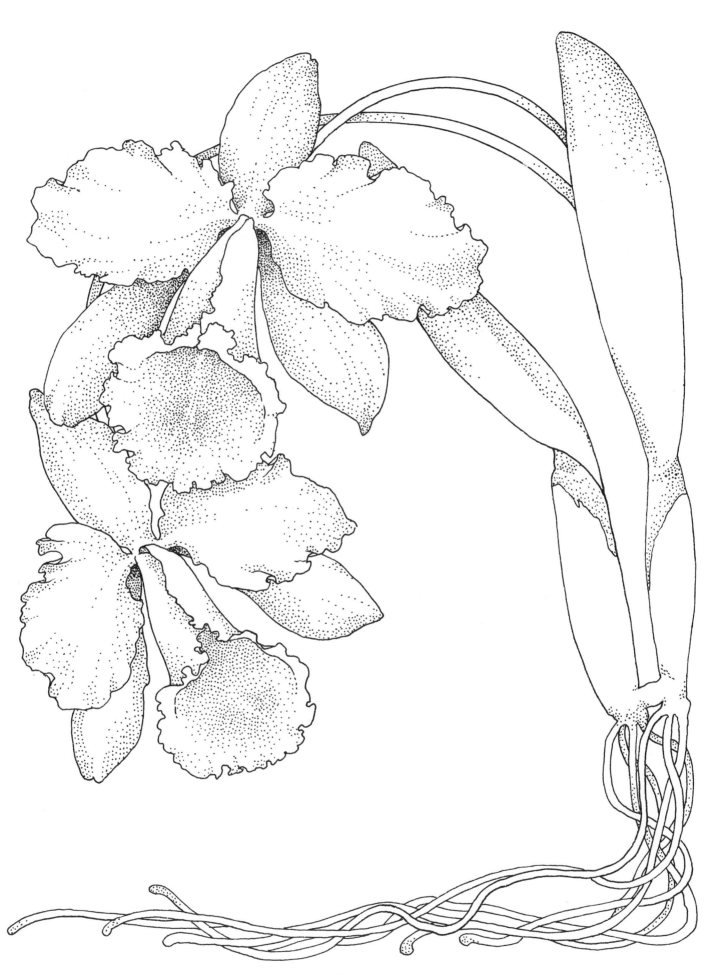

Orchid

Black-eyed Susan

Crocus

32

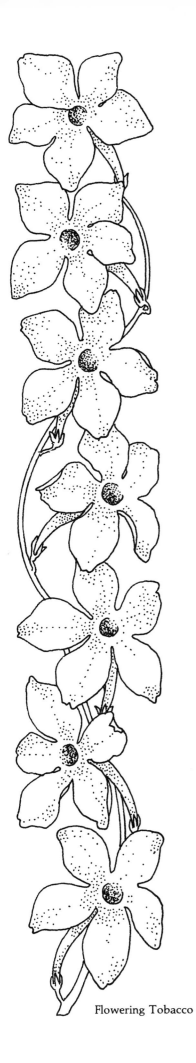

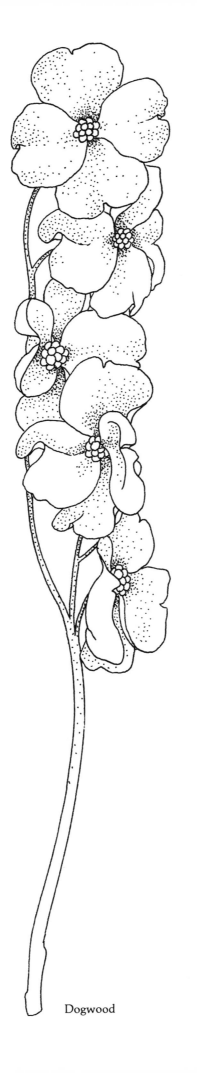

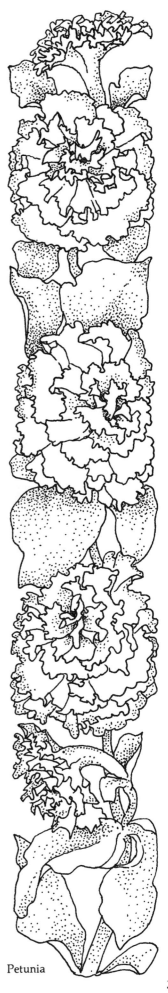

Flowering Tobacco   Dogwood   Petunia

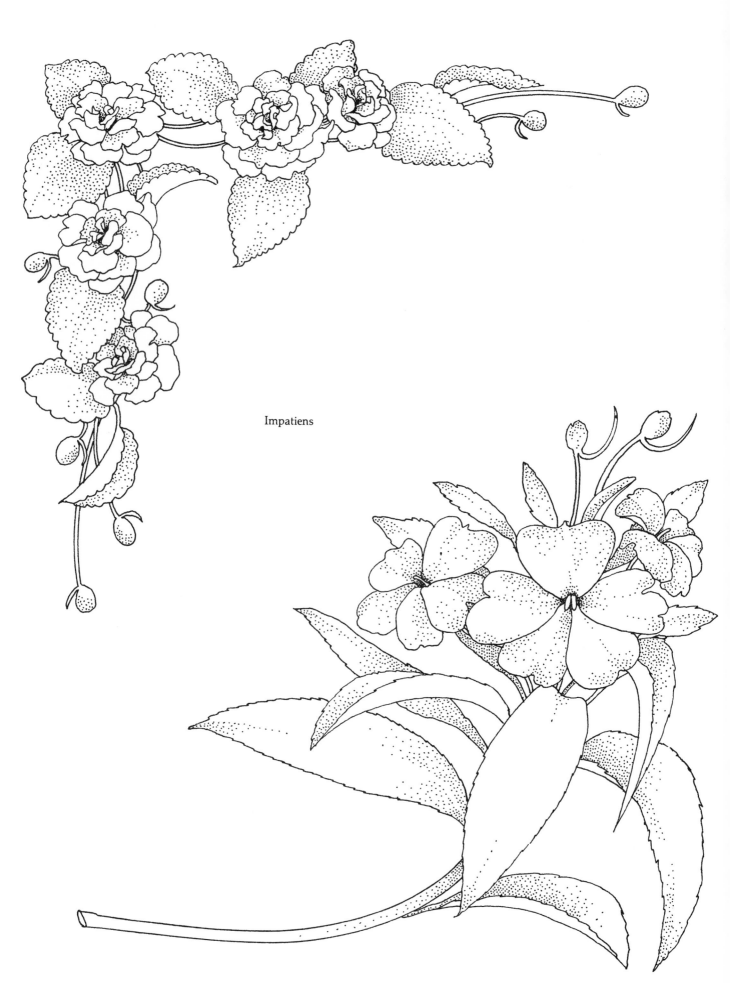

Impatiens

Marigold

Oxalis

Magnolia

Rhododendron

Nasturtium

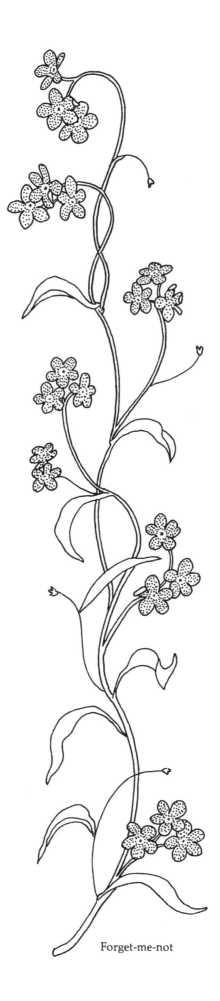

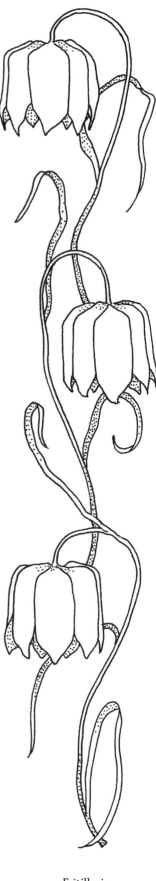

Christmas Cactus

Forget-me-not

Fritillaria

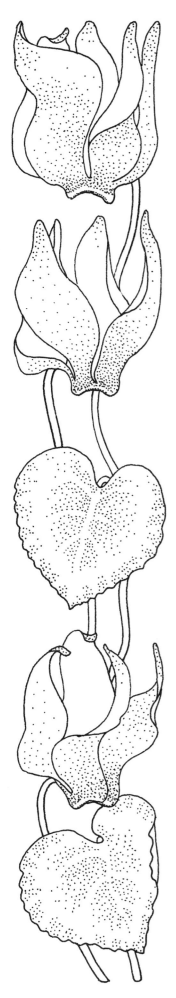

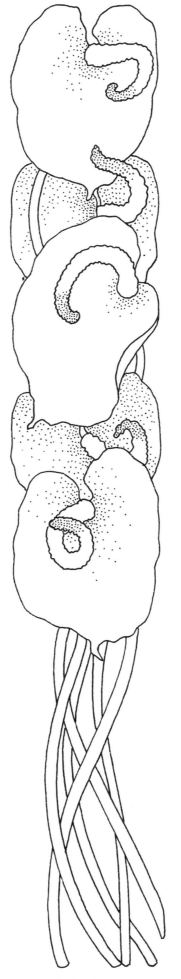

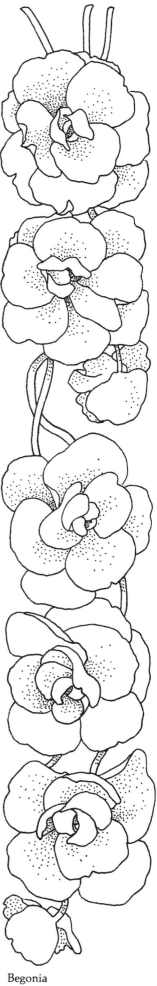

Cyclamen

Anthurium

Begonia

39

Flowering Quince

Ivy Geranium

Water Lily

African Violet

Coralbells

Primrose

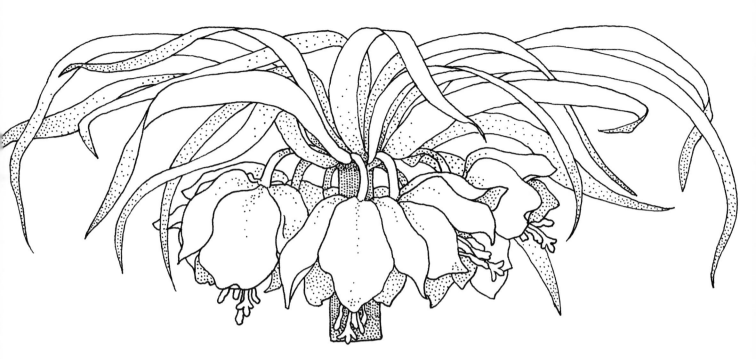

Fritillaria

Helenium

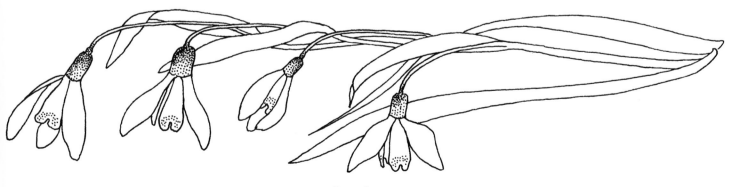

Snowdrop

Rose

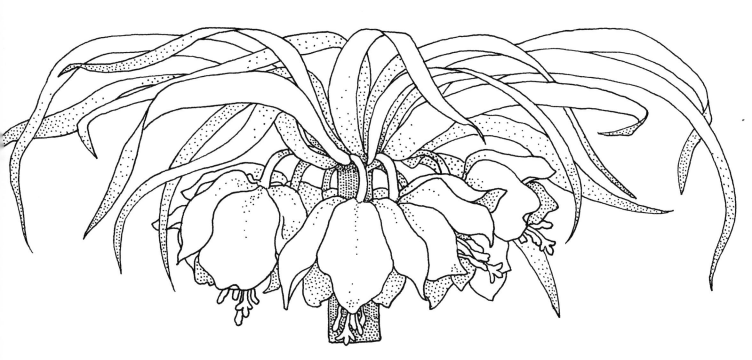

Fritillaria

Helenium

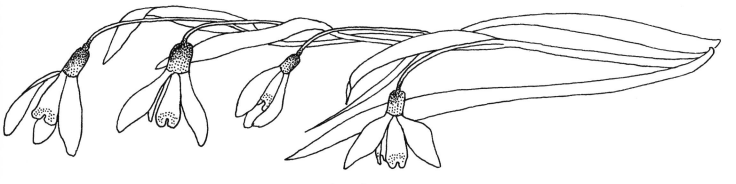

Snowdrop

Rose

Iris

Ranunculus

Strawflower

Sunflower

Gloxinia

48

Primrose

49

Asarina

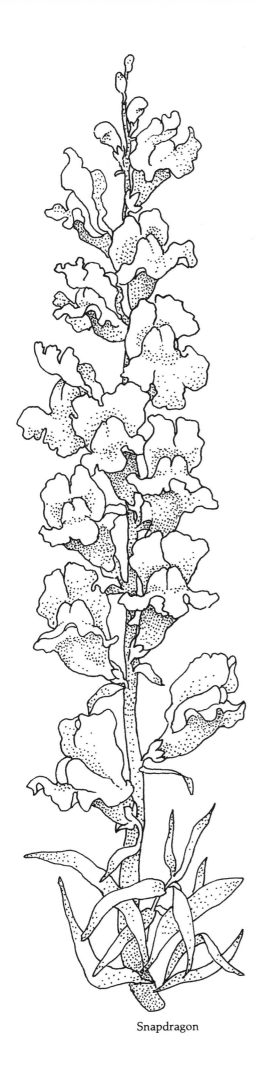

Snapdragon

Foxglove

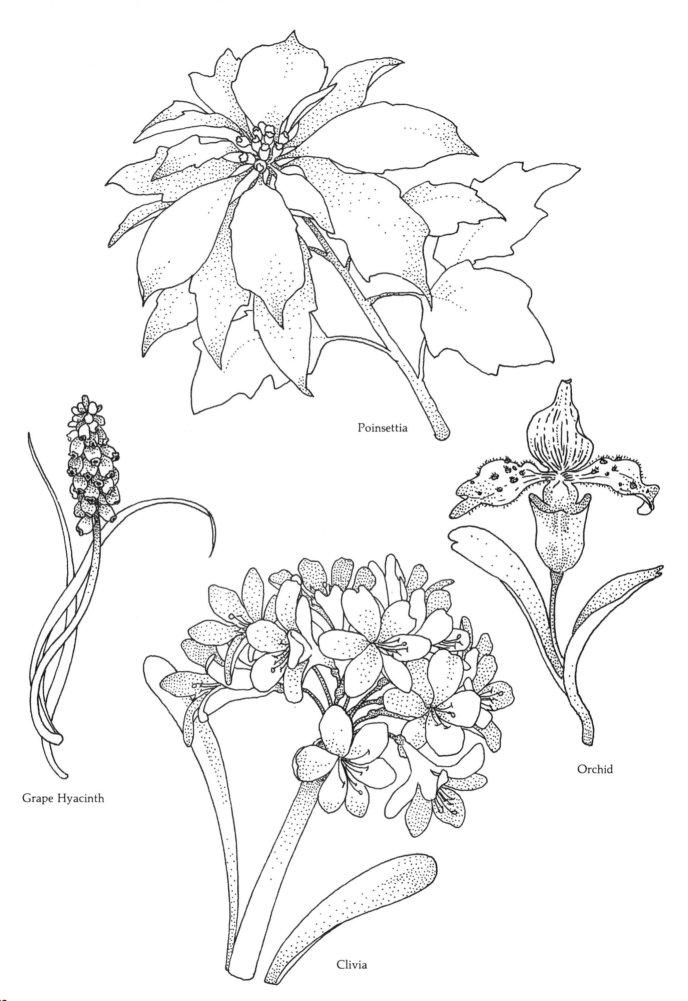

Poinsettia

Grape Hyacinth

Orchid

Clivia

Flowering Quince

Dianthus

Layia

Lilium

56

Freesia

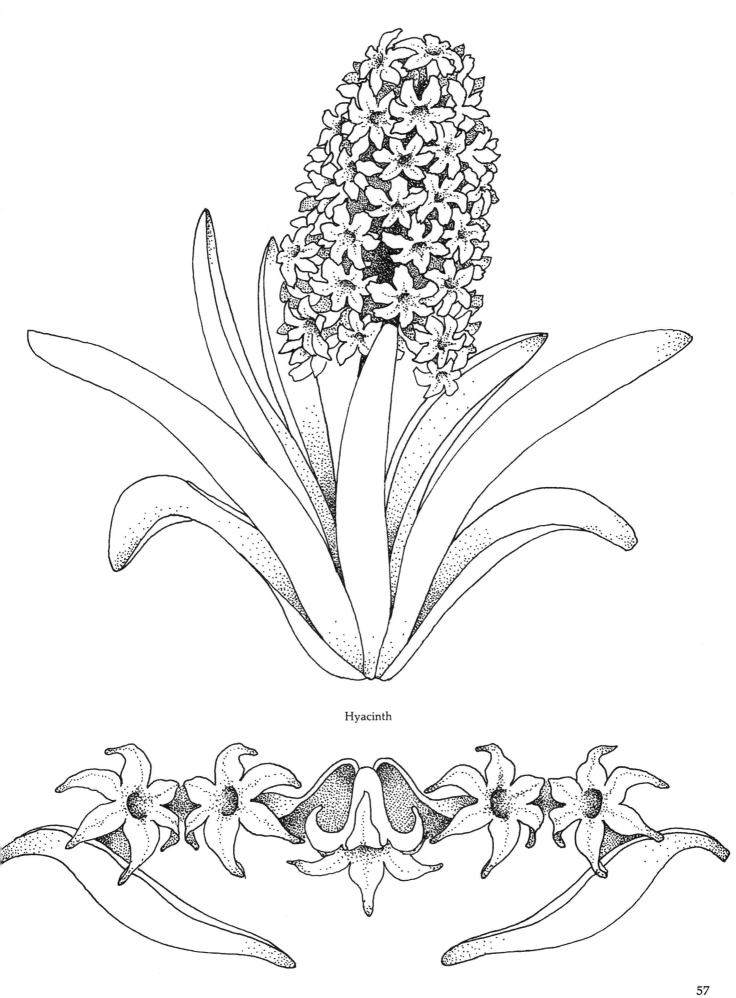

Hyacinth

Coreopsis

Iris

Verbena

Canterbury Bells

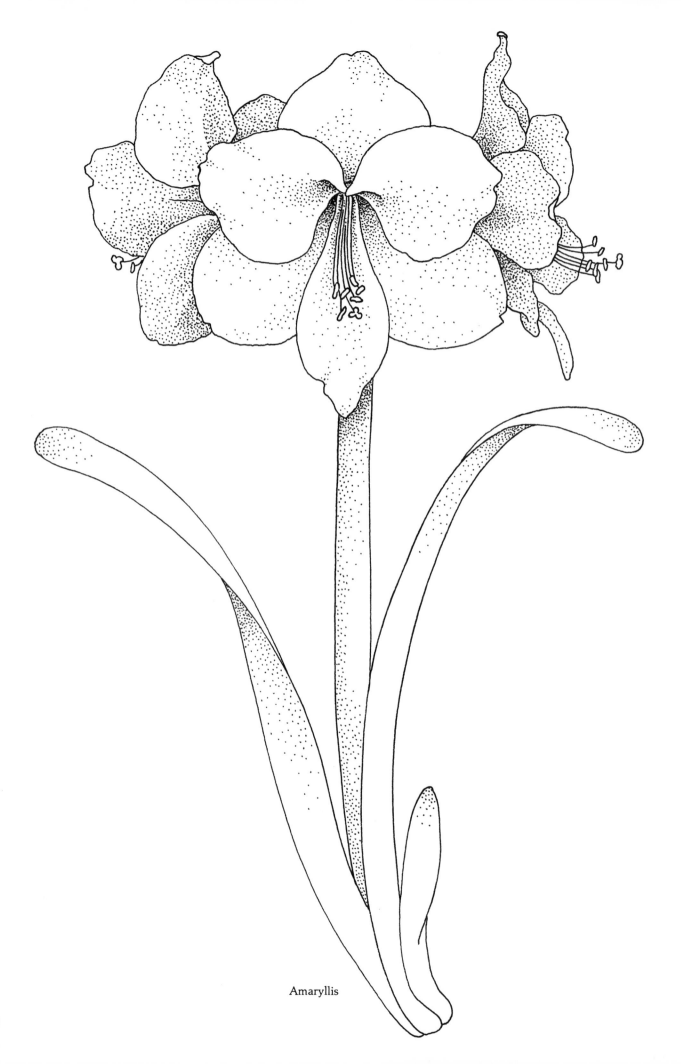

Amaryllis

Narcissus

Transvaal Daisy

Scabiosa

Calla Lily

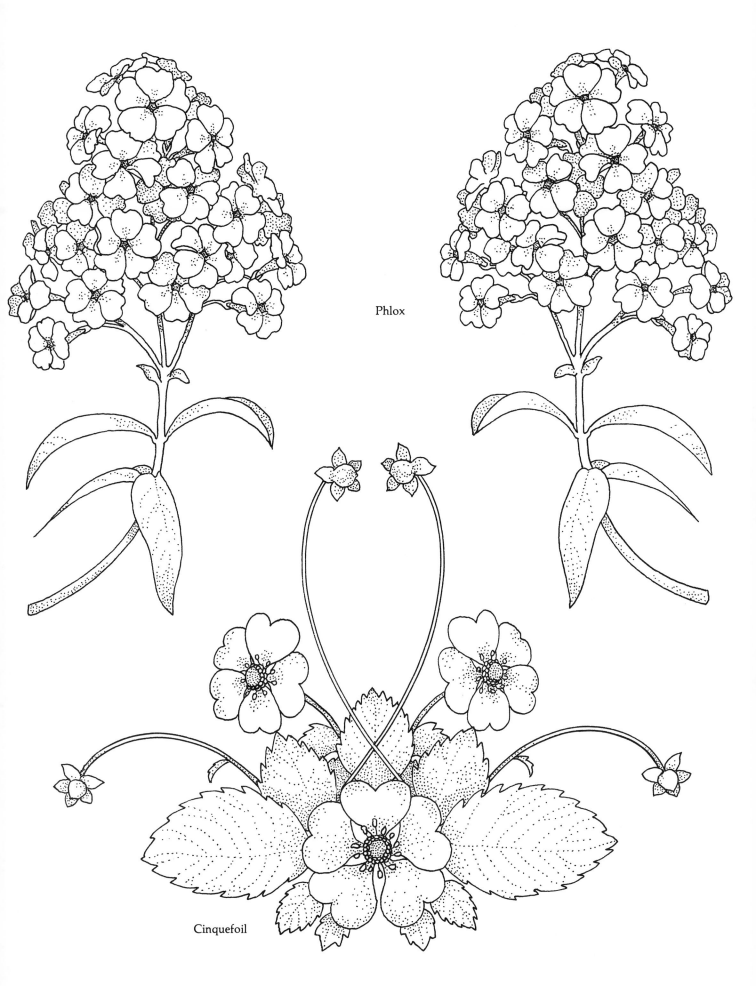

Phlox

Cinquefoil

Rose

Honeysuckle

Edelweiss

Sweet Pea

Daffodil

Viola

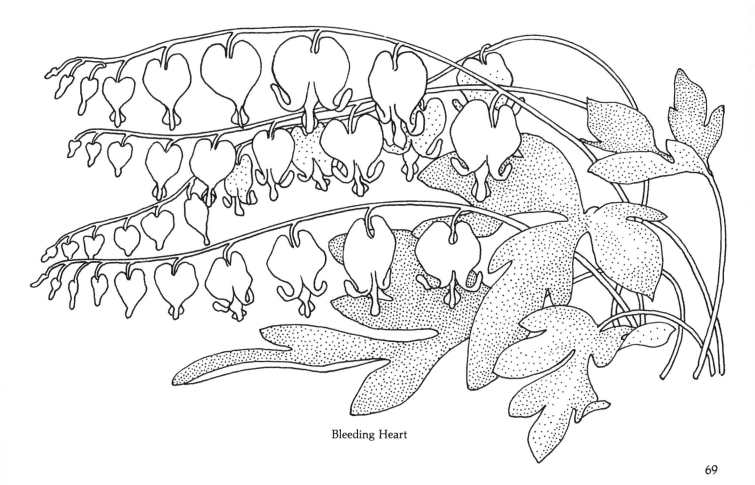

Bleeding Heart

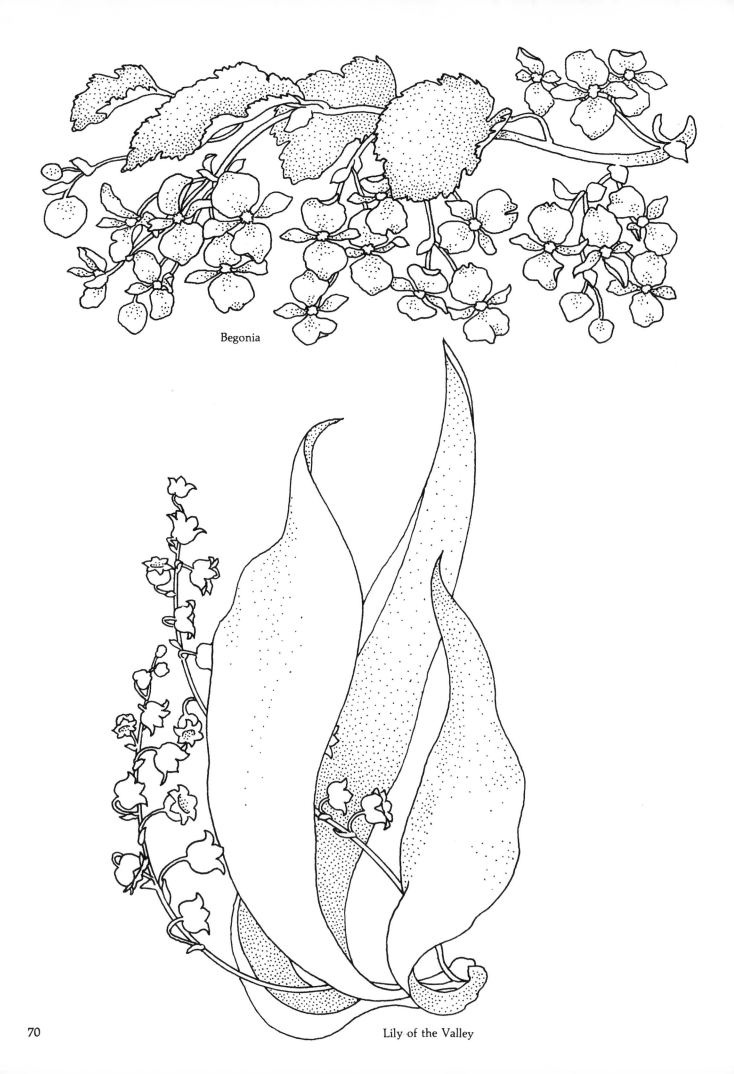

Begonia

Lily of the Valley

Rose

Chrysanthemum

Shasta Daisy

Hydrangea

Rose

Day Lily

Flowering Tobacco

Anemone

Daffodil

Camellia

Geranium

Rose of Sharon